Create Your Own Magic

By: Nikki Bryan

A Molding Messengers Publication

Create Your Own Magic

Copyright © 2020 by Ten'Niquwa Bryan

All rights reserved. Printed in the United States of America. No part of this book may be used or reproduced in any manner whatsoever without written permission except in the case of brief quotations embodied in critical articles or reviews.

This book is a work of fiction. Names, characters, businesses, organizations, places, events and incidents either are the product of the author's imagination or are used fictitiously. Any resemblance to actual persons, living or dead, events, or locales is entirely coincidental.

For information about permission to reproduce selections from this book, Write to Molding Messengers, LLC 1728 NE Miami Gardens Dr, Suite #111, North Miami Beach, FL, 33179 or email Info.Staff@MoldingMessengers.com

Library of Congress Control Number: 2020907404

Print ISBN: 978-0-578-68238-9

eBook ISBN: 978-0-578-68239-6

A Molding Messengers Publication

Create Your Own Magic

By: Nikki Bryan

A Molding Messengers Publication

Acknowledgements

I would like to acknowledge Yonie Dorval as she was the person that planted the idea in my mind to create this book after my Goals Party in January of 2019. She said to me, "I need a book of affirmations to read daily. You should write a book because I am sure that I am not the only one. I know you'll make it your own but do it." I started on it right away! She was also one of the six ladies who piloted this project with me. I would also like to acknowledge those ladies as well: Cynthia Ortiz, Perony Mertil, Shakiya Hunter, Shimeldine Delivra, and Tracy Midi. Thank you for holding me accountable for the first thirty days. Although we didn't get to complete the full sixty days, the fact that I did it with you ladies motivated me to get it done. Thank you all for journeying with me.

Preface

Without even noticing, every day I would say an affirmation. I would journal and intentionally act on it. As I went through many trials and tribulations, I would still do the same things. Continuing to do this routine, I realized that was how I was getting through the many storms. During the loss of my grandmother, through the loss of my daughter, through the failing of college classes, through the relationship dramas; these rituals got me through to the other side.

Always finding the greater things in life. Always manifesting the *dopest* magic into my life. After many years, I realized I was uncovering layers of myself through these routines, which then made me realize that the power was in my hands to create the very life I so desired, if I did it right.

As I began to do it "right", my business began to flourish; I became happy and free. The dead weight from relationships and friendships fell off and I began to flourish as a person.

I decided to write this book of affirmations to share with others how to create their own magic, how to manifest their own *dopeness* into their lives. After a lot of research, I found that there aren't many books about affirmations that aren't surrounding religion. Although I have nothing against religion, this is an amazing book that can benefit anyone no matter what faith they walk in.

The goal is for every reader to affirm, create, and manifest. Are you ready to create the life you desire?

Introduction

If you're looking for a daily book of affirmations that will transform your life, you've picked up the right book. Get ready for your life to go from okay to magical. Every day you'll be required to affirm, create, and then manifest. This book will teach you to love yourself before anything else. It will teach you to believe in yourself in every aspect. It will teach you how to manifest the smaller things in life which will in turn, create the bigger magic; the overall life you desire and deserve.

Within this book are tools and guidance on tapping into the divine being that exists within you. These affirmations will teach you to appreciate and nurture your soul and your life.

Are you ready to transform your life and create your own magic?

Get ready to:

-Affirm. Say the affirmation

-Create. Perform suggested exercise.

-Manifest. Reflect and move closer to the life you desire.

Self-Love

I am sure you've heard the cliché saying that self-love is the best love. Well it may be cliché but it's the best truth. Self-love is the foundation of everything, yet it is the hardest thing to obtain. Why? Well because we focus so much time on trying to love others while hating our own flaws and imperfections. Tell me, how does that even sound remotely correct. "I love you Johnny, you're perfect the way you are.", but to yourself, "Wow, I am fat and dark. I just hate myself for looking like this." Do you expect Johnny to love you if you don't love yourself?

Now I am not saying you can't dislike something about yourself, but do not dwell on them or make them the basis of your life. I am saying sometimes you have to love your imperfections and your flaws because they make you who you are. Don't speak hate, dissatisfaction, hurt, or anger into your own life. Love yourself enough to make the appropriate changes. You've got to love yourself beyond measure so that others can love you, and love you appropriately. You are worth loving unconditionally! You are worth taking yourself to a quiet day at the park. You are worth treating yourself after that promotion. You are worth embracing all of your 'perfections' because no mistake was made when you were created. You deserve your own divine and genuine love!

Before you pour out of your own glass, take a sip first. The goal is to love yourself, or nobody will!

Day 1

I am a PERFECT imperfection and I love every damn thing about me!

Today, embrace one of your imperfections. Every part of you deserves your love and attention. Don't you think so?

For me, it's my big eyes. Yes, my eyes are big but they're light brown and beautiful. I'm going to post a picture of social media of my favorite "imperfection"

Daily Reflection

Day 2

My body is my house. It is my source of energy and light 💡

*We use and misuse our bodies, sometimes to the benefit of others. Not realizing that our bodies are meant for **us**. It's meant to take us to where we need to go. How can we be so foolish to not love our bodies?*

Take a bubble bath, de-stress, give yourself a massage. Apologize to your body for mistreating it.

Daily Reflection

_____
_____
_____
_____
_____
_____
_____
_____
_____
_____
_____
_____
_____
_____
_____
_____
_____
_____
_____

Day 3

I think differently, but that is my superpower!

Too often we say I'm just going to be quiet because everyone doesn't think like me, or they won't understand. While that is true, YOU do think differently, that's your superpower. It's part of your purpose, it's that way to help you with YOUR vision.

Today, engage in a debate/discussion, play devil's advocate like you always do.

Daily Reflection

_____
_____
_____
_____
_____
_____
_____
_____
_____
_____
_____
_____
_____
_____
_____
_____
_____
_____
_____
_____

Day 4

I am no mistake; I am destined for greatness!

Sometimes, we forget who we are and who we're meant to be. We begin to stray from the path that was already destined for us. Stop and think, if there's a path already designed just for ME, why am I doing anything else? Why am I making it harder than it needs to be?

Today, do something that you've been holding off that would take you to the next level in your life.

Daily Reflection

Day 5

I am NOT a rib; I am a unique soul.

When I sit down and think about all the power that women possess; the mountains we can move, the ground we can break. There's absolutely no way that we are a PIECE of anyone. We are WHOLE. We are the unique souls meant to join forces WITH men. If any man can't recognize that, NEXT!

Today, write down any past relationship traumas, hurt, any insecurities, or any fear. Then burn the paper. The energy is right where it needs to be today.

Daily Reflection

_____
_____
_____
_____
_____
_____
_____
_____
_____
_____
_____
_____
_____
_____
_____
_____

Day 6

I don't shine every day but I'm still a diamond. ♦

Some days, we wake up feeling bummy, or like we're not progressing, like we're not it. But you are ALWAYS WORTH IT. It's time for you to stop discrediting yourself, it's time for you to celebrate every part of yourself. You're a diamond even in your sweats, hair tied, and bare face. YOU'RE IT!

Write down 3 things today that make you frown. When you reflect tonight, write 3 things that counter them.

Daily Reflection

_____
_____
_____
_____
_____
_____
_____
_____
_____
_____
_____
_____
_____
_____
_____

Day 7

I am a reflection of the universe and the universe is a reflection of me.

We've all heard, what you put out into the universe is what you get back, and to be honest, it's the truth. Whatever you put out into the universe; it's going to give it right back to you. Whether it be thoughts or actions. What are you putting out into the universe? Are you putting out what you want back?

Spend time in nature today. Listen to what it is saying to you. Meditate for ten minutes. Just listen!

Daily Reflection

_____
_____
_____
_____
_____
_____
_____
_____
_____
_____
_____
_____
_____
_____
_____
_____
_____

Day 8

My strength doesn't define, my perseverance does.

Odd thing to say, huh? Especially because you need strength to persevere but it's the truth. To have strength means that you were strong enough to withstand the pressure applied. But what about the aftermath? What about finding courage to keep going? That's perseverance! It's what you do after the pressure is applied, it says a lot about you!

Reach out to a friend today. Make sure they're okay. Whoever comes to mind, just reach out. They might need the courage to keep going.

Daily Reflection

_____
_____
_____
_____
_____
_____
_____
_____
_____
_____
_____
_____
_____
_____
_____

Day 9

Today I am going to love myself like I love everyone one else!

Very *often, we aim every day to love on others and make sure they have a good day, but we forget about ourselves, we forget to love ourselves. Then, we wait around for others to love us after we love them. Why should anyone love you if you aren't loving yourself?*

Show yourself some love today. Celebrate you!

Daily Reflection

Day 10

I am responsible for the energy I allow around me and I want nothing but positive energy!

Do you have that one person that every time they come around your entire energy shifts? But yet, you still call them. Okay, I get that Jason or Stephanie has been rocking with you since grade school but Jason and Stephanie are low vibrational beings and don't rock with you the way you think. You need to protect YOUR energy. You and only you are responsible for the energy around you; make it pure!

Today, write a list of things/triggers/actions/indicators that cause your energy to shift. Take a mental note of them because you're responsible for what happens next.

Daily Reflection

_____
_____
_____
_____
_____
_____
_____
_____
_____
_____
_____
_____

Day 11

I am more powerful than my nickname.

I'm a firm believer that there is power in our names, even common ones. But then we give, or we're given, nicknames, which essentially a shorter or simpler version of ourselves. Read that again. Nicknames are usually created for the convenience of others, not us. At some point we create an entire persona around this nickname and it's never 100% YOU! It's never as powerful as YOU!

You don't have to ditch your nickname; I use mine to maintain privacy and protection. But I address myself as Ten'Niquwa at least 5 times a day, especially during self-talk. Ten'Niquwa is so much more powerful than Nikki ♥

Daily Reflection

_____
_____
_____
_____
_____
_____
_____
_____
_____
_____
_____
_____
_____
_____

Day 12

My character is my currency!

How many times have you walked away from someone because they showed you their true character? Their character couldn't afford to be around you. How many times have you gotten something just because someone liked your character?

Today, express what your character has bought you or can buy you.

Daily Reflection

Day 13

I don't fake it until I make it, I *faith* it until I make it.

Fakeness and fear have no room in our lives. You should never fake something because that means you don't believe that it is yours already. Have faith that what you are seeking is already seeking you too. Keep the faith until you get where you are going.

Write down some things that you need to shift your energy on.

Daily Reflection

Day 14

Self-love is the best love!

Self-love is also the most important love because if you don't love yourself then how will someone else know how to love you? How will you know when someone else is loving you? Love yourself or no one else will!

Show yourself some love today. Treat yourself to massage, a lunch date, or just some quiet time.

Daily Reflection

Day 15

I'm not matching energy, but I'm not sacrificing mine!

Nowadays, people say, "I'm matching energies," but why would you want to match a low vibration? No! We're not doing that, what we are going to do is STOP SACRIFICING OUR ENERGY. We don't realize that's what we do when we entertain certain behaviors, we sacrifice our own energy and our own peace! Is it worth it?

Today, write down what causes you to sacrifice your energy. Then burn the paper and release the ashes into the air outside.

Daily Reflection

_____
_____
_____
_____
_____
_____
_____
_____
_____
_____
_____
_____
_____
_____
_____
_____
_____
_____

Day 16

I choose my peace above everything else!

Let's talk about your inner peace. Let's talk about how important it is for your sanity, your well-being, and your progression. Some people say risk it all or take a chance. But NOTHING is worth your peace. Once your peace is disrupted, everything else will be disrupted. You start missing out on blessings. So, it's never worth it. Choose YOUR peace every time!

Today, write down some things that disrupt your peace, then write down some things you do to regain your peace.

Daily Reflection

Day 17

I'm no longer selling myself for less than I'm worth. Full price or no deal!

You've sold yourself for less than you're worth, where has that gotten you? No more discounts, no more bargains. Increase your profit margin and add tax! Somebody has the currency to pay your worth. Pass up every offer until then. You know you're worth it, it's time you start acting like it.

Today, write down your worth and become one with.

Daily Reflection

Day 18

Today, I put myself first, second, third, AND fourth!

I'm sure you've heard the phrase, "You can't pour from an empty glass!" And you really can't. Too often we look to give others what we don't even have. We look to satisfy their every need and desire, but overlook our own. That shouldn't be the case. You have to put yourself first in order to successfully navigate through life. You have to know your own needs, wants, limits, standards, etc.; but before you can help/be there for someone else.

Do something for yourself today. Take a "me day".

Daily Reflection

Day 19

I am stronger than my strongest excuse.

We tend to make a lot of excuses for ourselves without realizing it. Some of our excuses are so strong that we convince ourselves not to do whatever it is we should be doing. But we're stronger than that. We are capable of overcoming our excuses. We have the power within us! Know that greatness is on the other side of our excuse.

Write down some of your most common/strongest excuses. What are some things you can say or do to combat those excuses?

Daily Reflection

Day 20

I am my own best friend, just as I am my own worst enemy.

We often forget the amount of power we have over our own lives. We forget that we are our first everything (or at least we should be). Just as we are our own best friend, we are our own worst enemy. We sometimes hurt ourselves without cause or we make bad decisions that put us in harm's way. It's time we start being our own best friend.

Today, choose to be your own best friend. Look out for your best interest. Make the right decision!

Daily Reflection

Manifestation

Manifestation. That's a word that has become extremely popular over the past few years, although, I believe many don't understand the true meaning of it. Manifestation originates from spirituality and/or religion. When something spiritual becomes real, it is a manifestation; a public display of emotion, feeling, or something theoretical made real. In short, manifestation is turning your hearts desires into real life. Who wouldn't want that?

The art of manifestation starts with belief. You have to first believe, or have faith, that it can and will happen. You have to believe in yourself, the universe, and the most-high. Manifestation doesn't work if you lack belief in any of the three. Think about it, we hear often that God has a particular life destined for us, yet we somehow end up living a completely different life. Why? Because we don't believe that we could live *that* particular life, we don't believe in ourselves. It doesn't mean that God or the universe wasn't ready to work in our favor. However, since we lacked the belief in ourselves, we couldn't manifest that particular life into existence.

I personally have been manifesting things into my life since elementary and middle school. My best friend and I would set out to write our goals annually. We would talk about all the things we wanted and wanted to happen. Then when the time came, we would say things like, "This opportunity is mine, no matter what!" Or, "I already have this scholarship in the bag." We would practice responses, "Ten'Niquwa, congratulations you got the job!" We would do all of these things in a joking manner, but little did we know we were actually assisting the universe in manifesting things into our lives.

This section of the book we are going to affirm, trust, and believe in one's self. You are going to learn how to manifest even the smallest things into your life. It all starts with belief!

Day 21

I trust myself!

Every morning, say this to yourself and every day MEAN IT. Trust your gut for it is your instinct, your angels guiding you, and God within you. The more you trust yourself, the more of what you want or need will become available to you. Know that you are equipped for it all, you just have to trust yourself.

Today, every chance you get just say, "I trust myself!"

Daily Reflection

_____
_____
_____
_____
_____
_____
_____
_____
_____
_____
_____
_____
_____
_____
_____
_____
_____

Day 22

I've been asking for an increase, but am I prepared for it?

Every day we ask for increase, we ask for more, but are we ready for it? Have you sat down and prepared for it? Mentally, physically, emotionally, financially, or spiritually? Are you ready for your mind to wonder on the days you want to give up? For your body to ache? For your emotions to be dismissed occasionally for the betterment of others? Are you prepared to go with less on some days to have an abundance in the end? Are you prepared for your spirit to be bothered and tested before you get to the finish line? Are you prepared for the next level?

What are you asking for increase on? If you haven't come up with a plan for when the increase arrives, do so today. Increase is on the way!

Daily Reflection

Day 23

My thoughts become my actions.

You're probably saying, "Nope, sometimes I think one thing and do the opposite." While that may be true, your thought process always has an influence on how you do things. Sometimes life throws us curve balls and our minds begin to wonder off on some of the worse things possible. We begin to overthink and accidentally THINK things into existence. Then we say, "I KNEW IT!" Well not really, you just thought it into existence. Your mind is just as powerful as your mouth. THINK exactly what you want to happen into existence, God/the universe is listening.

Today, before you do anything else, take 5-10 minutes to THINK how you want your day to go, down to the parking spot at the store.

Daily Reflection

_____
_____
_____
_____
_____
_____
_____
_____
_____
_____
_____
_____
_____
_____
_____

Day 24

You have to believe it first.

Anything that you want or need in your life starts with belief. You have to believe first that it is yours and you deserve it. If you don't believe in your heart then it will not come to you, it will not be drawn to you. Believe that you'll get that promotion. Believe that you'll get approved for that house. Believe that you will be healed. Believe that you'll gain peace.

What have you had doubt about recently? Write it down, cross it out, and write a belief statement instead.

Daily Reflection

_____
_____
_____
_____
_____
_____
_____
_____
_____
_____
_____
_____
_____
_____
_____
_____
_____
_____

Day 25

What's for me is for me, but let me secure it first.

We've all heard the infamous phrase, what's for me is for me. So, we begin to talk, or broadcast, and then when it doesn't happen for us, we say "Then it wasn't for me." While in some cases that could be true, most of the time, it's not. See, what's for you is for you but you have to manifest it into your life and actually have it. Until then, it's still out in the universe where it can be intercepted by someone else. Whether it be someone who just didn't want you to have it, or someone who felt they deserved it more than you. Yes, there are those types of people and just their THOUGHTS alone can intercept what was meant for you. It's yours goal, my friend, but secure it, THEN you can let it be known.

What are some things you know are meant for you? Write it down and meditate on it today.

Daily Reflection

_____
_____
_____
_____
_____
_____
_____
_____
_____
_____
_____
_____
_____

Day 26

Master the art of 'Shhh'.

Do you understand what that means? My grandmother used to say, "Work with your mouth shut," or "Never let your right hand know what your left hand is doing". As I mentioned yesterday, you've got to let things fully manifest into your life. Speaking about them prematurely to others can sometimes stop them from coming your way. I know when you're doing something exciting, or something you've always wanted to do, you want to call your mom or your best friend or spouse. However, you've got to master the art of being quiet, even with them. Sometimes they can unintentionally have bad vibes around them or just simply not understand your vision or say something that lowers your vibration towards whatever is happening. You do not have to talk about every move you're about to make with anyone, just make them!

Today, get a journal specifically for your goals. In this journal, you'll write about your goals and as you're manifesting them.

Daily Reflection

_____
_____
_____
_____
_____
_____
_____
_____
_____

Day 27

Once you ground yourself, all of the answers will come from within.

Have you ever just wanted a sign? Like, "God, just give me a sign if this is what you want me to do!" Yes, this has been all of us at one point or another, but when you pray for something and you're waiting for it to manifest into your life, what are you doing in the meantime? Are you meditating? Are you grounded enough to meditate? Praying is YOU speaking to the most-high, meditating is the most high speaking to you. You've got to be grounded, meaning you are relieved of stress, an open and clear mind, knowing and trusting your body and mind, and connecting with nature. Once you have learned to ground yourself, you'll realize that the answers to your prayers or questions have already been answered. Your answers come once you are still; mentally, physically, spiritually, or all at once.

Write down some things you've been praying about or questioning, then practice grounding yourself. I like to sit by a body of water and take deep breaths to ground myself before I meditate.

Daily Reflection

_____
_____
_____
_____
_____
_____
_____
_____
_____

Day 28

Let my mouth say what my heart reflects. May that manifest into my life.

We must become one with ourselves. Know that when you truly want to manifest things into your life, your heart, mind, and mouth must all reflect the same thing. If there is any conflict within you, there will be conflict around you. Train your body to be on one accord, everything you desire will gravitate to you.

Today, write any conflict that you may be experiencing within, then tonight, reflect on how you can change this.

Daily Reflection

Day 29

Speak what you seek until you see what you said!

How bad do you want it? If you want it that bad, remember that you have power in your tongue. Whatever you speak consistently ultimately becomes reality. Continue to speak what you are seeking until it's in front of your eyes, until it is in your life. You deserve it!

While in nature today, speak 3 things you are seeking to the wind. Say it with confidence!

Daily Reflection

Day 30

I am going to ask for exactly what I need, every day.

You owe yourself that much to ask for exactly what you need AND want. Make the decision to be done with selling yourself short by asking for small things, like, "God, just bless me with a $1000 to pay my bills this month!" Why not just ask for $10,000 to pay your bills, start a business, and bless someone else? Be direct, be specific, be honest, and ask for EXACTLY what you need and want.

Today, ask for EXACTLY what you need AND want!

Daily Reflection

Day 31

As it is within, may it reflect out.

Within yourself, you possess so much power and desire. You can manifest any and everything into your life. As long as you believe it within, it will materialize. Whether it's peace, success, love, or money.

Today, reflect on what's inside of you.

Daily Reflection

Day 32

As I open my heart, may the universe open up to me and for only me.

We've all heard the phrase, "Put out what you want to get back," and the golden rule, "Treat others the way you want to be treated." These phrases are usually followed by, "Even if others don't replicate the same, at least I know I did my part." Okay, so today you're going to retire that thought and any other similar thoughts. You're going to demand to receive what you put out. If you're opening your heart, let the universe do the same for you. If you're kind to others, let others be kind to you. Allow no room for anything else. You deserve to get back what you put out in the universe. You've just got to demand it back and you can do so in a humble manner.

Be specific and receptive in everything that you do today!

Daily Reflection

_____
_____
_____
_____
_____
_____
_____
_____
_____
_____
_____
_____
_____
_____

Day 33

I will start reaching out for success.

Success is within your reach, but only when you start reaching out for it. Little do we know; we create what's not there. Sometimes a seat at the table is already there, other times we have to reach and create the seat. Oh, and you're deserving of the seat so reach out for it!

Daily Reflection

Day 34

My thoughts create my reality; therefore, I will continue to consistently think of the life I want.

I know I've said it already, but you deserve the life you want. Because we know our thoughts become reality, let that consume your mind. Let exactly the life you want to live consume yourself. Let it become your reality. Be free of doubt, free of fear, be full of joy, full of prosperity, and full of peace!

Let go of any negative thoughts you may have today. Prepare for a new moon, a new day, and a new mind.

Daily Reflection

Day 35

Connect with the silence within you, it'll help make sense of what's disturbing you.

Most days, we have a million things going on, some of which are just distractions. Those distractions turn into disturbances and we don't even realize it. They disturb us to the point that we can't manifest the things we want into our lives because our vibe is off. We in turn call up everyone around us but never call on ourselves. On most occasions, we are our own best company. We possess the answers to our own problems within.

Make room at the table and sit with yourself today.

Daily Reflection

Day 36

I am a divine being, an all-powerful creator.

Most days, we forget how powerful we are. We have the power within us to create life into another being, a business, an idea, or even to create peace. Embrace it.

Today, take note of some things you have created.

Daily Reflection

Day 37

Nothing external to me has any power over me.

You have full control over your life and your surroundings. You have the power to block and protect yourself from negative energy. With that same power you have the ability to create the life you so desire, regardless of outside forces. Don't let anything or anyone stop your shine!

Today, write down a time you felt defeated by the outside world. Knowing what you know today, what would you do differently?

Daily Reflection

Day 38

Every intention sets energy in motion.

With every thought you think, it sets something into motion. Hence why I continue to tell you to think and speak of the life you want to live into existence. Be sure that your intentions are exactly what you want to happen, down to your mood. Yes, it's that important and it's that deep.

Today, just be intentional in everything that you do. Before you continue on with your day, decide right now how you want the rest of your day to go.

Daily Reflection

Day 39

Release all things that do not serve you and make room for all that does.

When manifesting the life that you desire, you should release everything that doesn't serve you. Why allow them to live rent free and they aren't beneficial to you? There is no sense in holding onto those things.

Today, write down all of the things that aren't serving you. Burn the piece of paper and release them back into the universe.

Daily Reflection

Day 40

I will stay consistent in manifesting the things I desire.

When manifesting the things, you want into your life, you must stay consistent. The things you are manifesting do not always come overnight or within a week. Sometimes it takes months or years. But as long as you stay consistent in asking for what you want, in due time it will come to pass.

Write down 3 things that you have not been consistent in asking for.

Daily Reflection

Create Your Own Magic.

In life we're handed so many things, so many challenges. Most days it feels like we're constantly running nonstop without taking in the moments. In our minds, we think we have a race to finish or our time is coming to an end of some sort. But like the late Nipsey Hu$$le said, life is like a marathon, you've got to pace yourself for it. You have to put the energy out that you want to get back and you have to speak all of the things you want into existence. This is how you create your own magic! There is a great plan destined just for you but you have to make the right choices to get it, to achieve it, and to live it. If you want magical things to happen in your life and to continue happening in your life, you have to create the space for it to be able to happen. When you wake up in the morning, set your intentions and decide, "I want magical things to happen to me today."

Creating your own magic requires your belief, your dedication, your persistence, and it requires you! Give it your absolute all. Be the very person you know you were created to be.

Create your own magic. You're already shining like it; you just don't see it yet.

Day 41

Today, I will go after everything I deserve and everything I desire.

Every day that you wake up and you live, you should spend every minute of that day doing something pertaining to your heart's desires. You should take every chance, every risk, every step towards the life that you deserve. Why should you settle? Why should you wait? Go for it!

Today, encourage someone else to go after their own desires.

Daily Reflection

Day 42

I am grateful for the vision I have been given. I am grateful for the life I am living!

When manifesting, you must always express gratitude. Be grateful for what you have and where you are for it is the stepping stone for what will manifest into your life next. Everyone always complains about the things that they don't have but never stop to appreciate what they do have. How can the universe trust you with "bigger and better" things if you don't appreciate the smaller ones? Learn to appreciate today because tomorrow isn't even promised!

What are you grateful for?

Daily Reflection

Day 43

I am ready for my marathon. I am equipped for my marathon.

Some days, I know it feels like you're in this never-ending race. You're tired, you're worn out, and you feel like this isn't the life for you. Like you don't have what it takes to make it to the finish line. But these are all lies. Don't operate in fear. Don't operate in defeat. You are equipped with everything for your marathon. It's not a race, you don't have to out run anyone, just do YOUR best. Life can be one hell of a run but keep going. It's always worth it. You're worth it!

Write your own affirmation. Something that relates to you, something that you can read to yourself when life gets difficult.

Daily Reflection

Day 44

My thoughts, my attitude, and my actions all align with my desired outcome.

In creating your magic, everything has to align with the greater good. If you truly want to become your own magic, your thoughts cannot be the opposite of your attitude or your actions. You would only be leading yourself to destruction.

Today sit down and write out your ultimate game plan.

Daily Reflection

Day 45

Stand for everything you believe in, be everything you believe in.

How bad do you want it? I said, how bad do you want it? What if I told you that all you had to do was just believe, then turn around and BE everything you believe in? What if I told you that's all it takes for you to receive everything you've been manifesting? Of course, you would do it, you'd believe! Belief starts with acceptance, accepting that what you're saying or doing is true. Acceptance that what you're asking for, but it is already yours! Whether it be peace or a range rover, believe that it is yours and it will be.

*Today, post a picture on social media of you **being** what you believe in.*

Daily Reflection

_____
_____
_____
_____
_____
_____
_____
_____
_____
_____
_____
_____
_____
_____
_____
_____
_____
_____
_____
_____

Day 46

I love myself; I trust myself; I believe in myself!

I know in order to do all three, it may have taken years to achieve. Some days you don't know if to trust yourself. Some days you find it hard to love yourself and even harder to believe in yourself. But if you can believe in others, if you can trust others, and show love to others, don't deprive yourself of the same. You have full control over you, you have power over you. If you love, trust, and believe in anyone, it should be yourself. You are an exceptional being, start treating yourself like it. Start living like it.

Today write a letter to yourself.

Daily Reflection

Day 47

I have an open mind and a burning desire.

Many were raised to wake up with certain expectations in mind. "The world isn't a kind place,", "People are racist, sexist, and prejudice,", or "The world is a concrete jungle,". While those things are factual, they are not law. Wake up with an open mind that there are many other positive things in the world. If you focus your energy on those things, you'll attract them and cause everything else to be insignificant. Attract it with a burning desire, attract it with intentions of making a difference.

Today, on one of your social media platforms, post about how you would like to change the narrative in your own life.

Daily Reflection

Day 48

The problems of the world are not me.

The problems of the world are not your burdens to carry unless you have a solution to fix them. Do not allow the problems of the world to consume so much of your attention. Value your peace so much, that you only focus on what is in front of you. Some might say that you have to care about what's going on around you and you should., but do not allow it to interrupt your peace. I am a firm believer that the most-high will put what he wants you to deal with in front of you. Everything else should fall to the waist side. We all came here with a purpose and not one person can fix every problem. Therefore, you should only give energy to the things that you have strength or knowledge to fix. Don't miss your blessings on YOUR path trying to fix something on someone else's path.

Write 3 things that you can contribute to.

Daily Reflection

_____
_____
_____
_____
_____
_____
_____
_____
_____
_____
_____
_____
_____
_____
_____
_____
_____
_____
_____
_____

Day 49

My soul will lead the way!

As I have mentioned before, our souls are us. Our bodies are just vessels to carry our soul during our time on this plane. So long as we allow our soul to lead the way, we will discover who we are underneath and we'll be able to create the life we desire easily. Learn who is truly in control.

Today, peel back another layer of self, describe your soul.

Daily Reflection

Day 50

Be like Nehemiah; leave the crowd!

In the 3rd grade, I read the book of Nehemiah in the bible. Nehemiah was this noble character that was called to rebuild the walls of Jerusalem. He went forth to do so, but it seemed to be the "uncool thing" to do. But Nehemiah didn't care, he followed his own mind and rebuilt the walls of Jerusalem. Even when they came to distract him from his good work, he didn't budge. Nehemiah left the crowd and stayed his course. You don't have to "break" the rules, but create your own.

What are some rules you have created for yourself?

Daily Reflection

Day 51

Visualize your success, visualize the life you desire.

I am really big on visualization! If you can see your dreams and your desires before you, how will you know what it looks like? How will you know when you achieve it? You've got to visualize and you've got to visualize every single day.

If you haven't created a vision board, start creating one today.

Daily Reflection

Day 52

Live the life of who you desire to be. Let it dominate your entire being.

If you haven't started, start assuming the feeling of your wishes fulfilled. If you want to live a happy life, start living a happy life. If you want to have a $60,000 job, start living like it. I know you're probably wondering, "Well how in the world do you presume I do that?" I know that you don't have the $60,000 yet but start making decisions as such. For $60,000 a year, it may require going to bed at 9 P.M. and be up at 5 A.M. Before the $60,000 arrives, assume this schedule. It is a form of inviting it into your life as well as mentally preparing your mind and body for the change.

Today, write seven things you can do to assume the life you desire.

Daily Reflection

Day 53

I am not worried about the how, I have already delegated that authority to life itself.

Manifesting the life that we desire is already a task within itself. The number one rule I have learned about manifesting is to set it and forget it. Trust that life will take care of the how, and it will all come together. Once again, you have to believe that the favor reserved for you in the universe will come into play. Believe that the most-high will deliver on your request. Therefore, do not worry about the how, better yet, do not worry at all.

At the end of the day, do a calming exercise for five to ten minutes.

Daily Reflection

Day 54

I place faith in myself and not into things.

Society has conditioned us to think or believe that we are nothing without something or someone else. I am here to tell you that isn't true. You are of value with or without anything or anyone else. No one thing or person is 100% loyal to you, therefore you've got to be 100% loyal to yourself. You've got to have faith in your entire being. Trust yourself. Trust your capabilities, trust your own hands, and trust your own mind. Have faith that you are a divine being.

Write a letter to yourself.

Daily Reflection

Day 55

Whatever I write will come to life. Whatever I speak will come to pass.

I can only speak from ongoing experience. Whenever I want or need to make a vision or goal my reality, I start by writing it out. For example, graduate school. I remember applying on the 23rd, then submitting all of my required documents by the 28th. But no one contacted me. By the 30th, I took it upon myself to continuously call until I got a hold of someone who could help. Finally, that day at 11:24 A.M., the person who was in charge of admissions told me, "Okay, we have all that we need. Hopefully within 2-3 days you'll have an answer and might be able to start the summer semester." Well the summer semester was set to start the following week and that is when I wanted to start. Once I disconnected from the call, I got my journal and wrote my acceptance letter. Three hours later, I received an email in the same style, accepting me into the university. Whether you are writing or speaking, so long as you believe it is yours, it is yours!

Today, write it out. Make it plain. Believe!

Daily Reflection

Day 56

I am done defining what my life should be, I am creating what my life will be.

We spend so much time defining our lives. "My life will be so much better if I did this or had that, or once I get this, I'll be happy." We should invest our time creating the life we want and actually enjoying it and appreciating it. Obviously, we have to know what we want out of life, but sometimes what we want it's how it's going to be or it won't come how we want it to come, and that is okay. Create your own freaking magic along the way and embrace it.

Today, do something you've never done before as long as it aligns with the life you're creating.

Daily Reflection

Day 57

Establish your lane. Create it with quality so it doesn't get lost.

Did you know that we were all created with our own life paths? A path specifically for us and our abilities, our personalities, our character often times we get led astray, doing things that others suggest thinking it'll yield us more money or higher status. But in reality, if it's not our path, it will never go the way they say it will. Usually it's more destructive and depressing. You should always walk your path, nourish your lane, jazz it up, and make it with great quality. The more we walk our destined path, the happier we are and the easier it becomes to manifest the things you want or need into your life.

Do you know your path? Map it out today. How are you going to create it with quality?

Daily Reflection

Day 58

Stay the course; overnight success can take 10 years.

I am constantly reminding myself that nothing happens overnight. I have full confidence in myself and my abilities. Therefore, I am training to set it and forget it. Set my intentions, make my visions plain and clear. Then, I am putting in the work, trusting and knowing that it will all come to pass. Whether it is two years or ten years. I believe and I know that it will come to pass.

Today, pay attention to your actions. Are you staying the course? Are you believing in yourself?

Daily Reflection

Day 59

Stay true to yourself and the universe will reward you.

Now that you're walking your path, it becomes easier to stay true to yourself. You take care of you, you appreciate you. Do you know what happens when you love yourself or when you appreciate yourself? That's correct, the universe starts to do the same to you and the people around you start to do the same thing. You begin to reap ALL of the benefits and all of the things you deserve.

Today, even in adversity, stay true to yourself!

Daily Reflection

Day 60

Create your own magic. You're already shining like it!

One of my major life lessons thus far is that many people see who you are long before you do. With that comes many blessings but also much envy. Sometimes people can't stand the thought of seeing you shine. They can't stand the thought of you coming into your true purpose and walking your path. Many times, because of this, we dim our shine. But that stops today. You know who you are. You know what you're capable of. You know your worth. You know your purpose. You know your path. You are loved and you are blessed. You are protected. You are a divine being. You shine everywhere that you go. Continue to create your own magic, the universe is depending on you for it.

Today, CREATE YOUR OWN MAGIC.

Daily Reflection